Irish Inspirations

Toasts, Wit & Blessings

STERLING INNOVATION
An imprint of Sterling Publishing Co., Inc.

New York / London
www.sterlingpublishing.com

STERLING, the distinctive Sterling logo, STERLING INNOVATION, and the Sterling Innovation logo
are registered trademarks of Sterling Publishing Co., Inc.

Library of Congress Cataloging-in-Publication Data Available

2 4 6 8 10 9 7 5 3 1

Published by Sterling Publishing Co., Inc.
387 Park Avenue South, New York, NY 10016

© 2009 by Sterling Publishing Co., Inc.

This book is comprised of material from the following Sterling titles:
Irish Cures, Mystic Charms & Superstitions © 1991 by Lady Wilde
Irish Folk Wisdom © 1993 by Mairtin O'Griofa
Irish Toasts, Curses, & Blessings © 1995 by Padraic O'Farrell
Irish Proverbs © 2000 by Fionnuala Carson Williams

Distributed in Canada by Sterling Publishing
c/o Canadian Manda Group, 165 Dufferin Street
Toronto, Ontario, Canada M6K 3H6
Distributed in the United Kingdom by GMC Distribution Services
Castle Place, 166 High Street, Lewes, East Sussex, England BN7 1XU
Distributed in Australia by Capricorn Link (Australia) Pty. Ltd.
P.O. Box 704, Windsor, NSW 2756, Australia

Printed in Singapore
All rights reserved

Sterling ISBN 978-1-4027-6340-3

For information about custom editions, special sales, premium and
corporate purchases, please contact Sterling Special Sales
Department at 800-805-5489 or specialsales@sterlingpublishing.com.

Contents

Toasts, Curses & Blessings

General Blessings

n today's busy society, it is difficult to realize that not so many years ago, little of our everyday business was undertaken without the benefit of God's blessing invoked by ourselves or others. Going to fish or save turf, hearing news of a death or marriage, consoling neighbors in sorrow or sharing their joy— there was a particular blessing for every occasion and people uttered these exclamations without fear of being considered passé or overly-religious. Some of these habits have survived. The simple "God bless you," "God save you," or "God rest his soul" are heard as often as they are mocked, at least.

Many of the following blessings are translated from the Irish; others are remembered from a rural childhood. All have their own charm and place in today's society.

HEALTH & WELFARE

May you live as long as you want and
never want as long as you live.

May you only grow old in the face,
be treasured and cared for with grace.

Peace on your hand and health to all who shake it.

If God sends you on a stony path,
may he give you strong brogues *(shoes)*.

If you have tears, may they turn God's mill wheel.

Whatever takes longest to come to you,
may it be worth waiting for.

Light in your eyes,
Teeth in your mouth,
Thatch on top.
Flesh on you,
Bone on you,
Legs and feet under you,
And a tail behind to guide you.

That the face of all good news and
the back of all bad news be toward you.

The Lord keep you in his hand
but never close his fist too tight on you.

Saol fada agus breac-shláinte chugat.
(Long life and middling health to you.)

Mary and her son, Brigid and her cloak,
God and His strength between you and pestilence.

Bless you and your clan and may every
limb of your body be as strong as Fianna's stick.

May springtime never be far away for you.

My thousand blessings and God's blessing on you,
and may you never want for anything.

The face of life and health and the beating of all be yours.

Christ walked on the rock.
A horse's foot was injured.
He put blood to blood,
Flesh to flesh, bone to bone.
As he cured that,
May he cure this.

God bless the mark.
*(Said upon noticing some
defect or disability.)*

May you always have food, clothing,
and a pillow for your head.

Seven times the full of St. Patrick's graveyard,
Seven times the full of the tomb of Christ,
Seven times the full of the well of grace,
Of blessings on you until we see each other again.

God save you, my three brothers! God save you!
How far have you to go?
To Mount Olivet, for gold for a cup to hold the tears of Christ.
Then go! Collect the gold, and may Christ's tears fall on it and
you will be cured in body and in soul.
*(Said while giving a drink to
a person with a stitch in his side.)*

May your barn be always full,
Free from fox and crow and gull.

Glory be to God on high.
Only for the bit we ate we'd die!

May you never bear the heavy load of an empty stomach.

May you have rye bread to do you good,
Wheaten bread to sweeten your blood,
Barley bread to do you no harm,
And oatmeal bread to strengthen your arm.

The five loaves and the two fishes of the five thousand
be with God's people always.

Prayer and fasting are good for a sinner,
But a hungry man would want his dinner.

A blessing will not fill the stomach,
but take it anyhow.

May there never be a rattle in your skillet.

May you never see the bottom of your pot.

May your griddle may always be hot.

May you escape the gallows, avoid distress,
and be as healthy as a trout.

Sláinte an bhradáin agat.
(Health of the salmon to you.)

To the doctor may you never hand any money,
and sweet be your hand in a pot full of honey.

Sláinte na bromaí agat.
(The strength of the colt to you.)

Long life and salvation to you.
May you stay alive,
healthy, and protected from harm.

God save you, Archangel Michael! God save you!
What ails you, man?
A headache, an ailment, and a heart weakness,
Archangel Michael; can you cure me, angel of the Lord?
May three things cure you, man:
May the shadow of Christ fall on you;
May the garment of Christ swathe you;
May the breath of Christ breathe on you.
And when I call on you again you will be cured.
*(Said over a patient while sprinkling water on his
head as his arms are raised to a cruciform.)*

May I see you gray and combing your children's hair.

God between us and all harm.

May Peter take, may Paul take, may Michael take the pain away,
the cruel pain that kills the back and the life, and darkens the eyes.
*(Written on paper which is tied to a hare's foot to be
worn by someone suffering from pain.)*

God rest Paul's soul.
*(Said when passing between a patient and the fire to prevent
catching the disease.)*

May you have a gentleman for a landlord.

May God give you your share of food and the
Host as long as you live and your family after that.

May God give you the back to bear the burden.

May the strength of three be in your journey through life.

God's help be always nearer than the door for you.

HOME

Céad mile faílte romath.
(A hundred thousand welcomes to you.)

God save all here bar the cat.
*(Said upon entering a house. It was considered
unlucky to bless the cat.)*

God bless the corners of this house,
And be the lintel blessed.
Bless the hearth, the table too,
And bless each place of rest.
Bless each door that opens wide
To stranger, kith, and kin;
Bless each shining windowpane
That lets the sunshine in.
Bless the rooftree up above.
Bless every solid wall.
The peace of man, the peace of love,
The peace of God on all.

Bless my humble kitchen,
Lord, I love its every nook.
Bless me as I toil in it
About my daily work.
Bless the meals that I prepare.
Grant seas'ning from above.
Bestow thy blessing and thy grace
And most of all, your love.
As we prepare to eat our meal,
May you the table spread,
Let us not forget to thank you, Lord,
For all our daily bread.
So bless my humble kitchen, Lord,
And all who enter it;
Bless them with joy and peace and love
As happily they sit.

May the blessing of the five loaves and two fishes that
God divided among five thousand be ours, and may the King
who divided place potluck in our food and in our portion.

I bank down this fire with the miraculous
powers that Patrick got.
May the angels pile it, may no enemy pull it apart.
May God make a shelter of our house
For all inside,
For all outside.
The sword of Christ over the door,
Until the light of day tomorrow.

God guard this home from roof to floor.
The Twelve Apostles guard the door;
Four good angels round each bed,
Two at the foot and two at the head.

Mary, who with tender ward
Did keep the home of Christ the Lord,
And did set forth the bread and wine
Before the living wheat and vine,
Please be beside me as I go
About my labors, to and fro'.
Speed the wheel and speed the loom
And guide the needle and the broom.
Make my cakes rise sweet and light,
Cure my cheese a creamy white.
Yellow may my butter be
Like cowslips growing in the lea.
Guard my skillets big and small,
Fill them with good food for all.
Guide my needles and my wool,
Keep my larder safe and full.
To me your gracious help afford,
Oh holy handmaid of the Lord.

Love & Marriage

May your love knot be sealed with heaven's wax.

Help and deliverance and friendship of God on you both.
God grant you a *gradle* of joy.
(Wedding blessing. Gradle means "great deal.")

May your peltin' paper be a hundred pound note.
(Document of consent to marry from a priest.)

May your partner be his own man to the power of two.

May the king's evil be cured for you.
*(Said as someone is blessed with water from a well
near the Boyne River, where King James is said to
have washed his sword after the battle.)*

Guím grásta ort.
(I wish grace on you.)

You for me and I for thee and never another.
Your face turned to mine and away from all others.
(Said secretly by a woman after offering a drink to her man.)

May the health that got you for us leave you healthy with us,
with the help of God and the light of his grace.
(Said by a couple when their child is born.)

The blessing of the saints and angels,
The blessing of anyone else who knows us;
And my own blessing, without stain, to you
Until the Kingdom of Glory.
(Said at betrothal.)

A golden ring on your swollen body.
(Said to a pregnant woman.)

May you never marry a whistling woman.
(Regarded as evil.)

Go maire sibh bhur saol nua.
(Marriage congratulation: May you enjoy your new life.)

That your wife may knit for infants and may her needles always
click after dark.
*(Such knitting was thought to be best because sheep were
asleep then.)*

May your bodies please each other
like the stars do their Master.

That your body will not cease
Its awareness of mine;
That your love continues to follow my face
As the calf follows the cow
From this day to the day of my death.

Sweet be her hand on you as if it came out of a pot of honey.

May your man never rise from an unfinished mass, from food without offering grace, or from yourself for another woman.

May you never be sent to the gander paddock
(May you never be in your wife's bad graces.)

Love, life, and happiness; may your troubles be few and your blessings plenty.

Sliocht sleachta ar shliocht bhur sleachta.
(May there be a generation of children on your children's children.)

DEATH

May I never kill a person and may nobody kill me.
But if someone thinks of killing me, may I kill him.

Ar dheas Dé go raibh a anam.
(May his soul be on the right hand of God.)

God's blessing be on the souls of the dead and
may we be a long time following them.

May God grant you a generous share of eternity.

May it be that you are never left to die a sinner.

Blessed Virgin, God's own mother,
Shining light set up on high,
Candle blazing in the heavens, be with me the day I die.

May the grass on the road to hell grow long.

Oh Brigid, Mary of the Gael,
Oh Brigid, extend your aid;
Keep me under your protection from all harm
Until I die in the companionship of God.

Blessed Mary, queen of grace,
Look after my soul every hour of each day,
When it passes beyond my cold, weak body.

May heaven be your bed.

May God level the road for your soul.

May you have a smith's
meitheal *(a big crowd)* at your wake.

When you reach the inn of death, I hope it's closing time.

May there be rain at your funeral.
(Considered a good omen.)

May you receive mercy and grace; death without sin; and may the
righteous gone before you receive their share of eternal glory.

May you and yours be furthest from the grave.

Self-Blessings

I lie with God; may he lie with me.

May sin and loss be kept from me during the course of this day.

May I be kissed by all in red petticoats and
check aprons between Kenmare and Killarney.
May I always meet my fetch at morning.

Kindle inside my heart, O Lord,
The spark of love
For my enemies, relatives, and friends.

May Jesus be at my head,
The Virgin at my feet,
The Twelve Apostles round my bed
When I am fast asleep.

There are four corners on my bed
And over them four angels spread:
Matthew, Mark, Luke, and John.
God bless the bed that I lie on.
If any evil comes to me,
O Holy Mary, waken me.
O God, I give my soul to Thee.

Jesus the branch and Mary the flower.
Jesus and Mary be with me all hours.

May the name of Jesus be firmly
inscribed in the middle of my heart.

Long eaters are long livers, so let not
my dinner be over before I get it.

May God's bounty and St. Patrick's blessing be with me.

That I may have the richness of health and know it.

If my neighbor has knowledge,
let me not be too proud to light my candle from it.

Between us and the little people,
Us and the people of the wind,
Us and the evil hour of temptation,
Us and the drowning power of water,
Us and the earth's withering breath,
Us and the slave's cruel death.
(Said before undertaking a journey.)

May I never take life too seriously,
knowing I'll never get out of it alive.

Blessings from the Poets

Céad Míle Faílte romhat,
Faílte is fiche romhat,
Naoí gcéad míle fáilte romhat,
Eileen Aroon.
*(One-hundred thousand welcomes to you,/Twenty-one welcomes to
you,/Nine-hundred thousand welcomes to you, sweet Eileen.)*

Bless this house, O Lord we pray.
Make it safe by night and day.
Bless these walls so firm and stout,
Keeping want and trouble out.
Bless the roof and chimneys tall.
Let thy peace lie over all.
Bless the doors that they may prove
Ever open to joy and love.
Bless the windows, shining bright,
Letting in God's heavenly light.
Bless the hearth ablazing there
With smoke ascending like a prayer.
Bless the people here within,
Keep them pure and free from sin;
Bless us all that we may be
Fit, O Lord, to dwell with thee.
Bless us all that we, one day,
May dwell, O Lord, with thee.
(Helen Taylor, Bless This House)

The blessing of a poor old man be with you night and day,
The blessing of a lonely man whose heart will soon be clay;
'Tis all the Heaven I'd ask of God upon my dying day –
My soul to soar forevermore above you, Galway Bay.
(Francis A. Fahy, "Galway Bay")

God bless my home in dear Cork city,
God bless the cause for which I die.
("The Dying Rebel")

Kidney of Bloom, pray for us
Flower of the Bath, pray for us
Mentor of Menton, pray for us
Canvasser for the Freeman, pray for us
Charitable Mason, pray for us
Wandering Soap, pray for us
Sweets of Sin, pray for us
Music without Words, pray for us
Reprover of the Citizen, pray for us
Friend of the Frillies, pray for us
Midwife Most Merciful, pray for us
Potato Preservative against Plague and Pestilence, pray for us.
(James Joyce, Ulysses)

Ye powers who over love preside!
Since mortal beauties drop so soon,
If ye would have us well supplied,
Send us new nymphs with each new moon!
(Jonathan Swift, "The Progress of Beauty")

O sages standing in God's holy fire
As in the gold mosaic of a wall,
Come from the holy-fire, perne in a gyre,
And be the singing masters of my soul.
(W. B. Yeats "Sailing to Byzantium")

AMUSING BLESSINGS

If I bless you with a song
That's not short and not too long,
It's 'cause quite often I wander a bit off key.
If the air causes alarm,
It will not do you much harm
'Cause the penance might save you from purgatory.

Many happy returns of the day and
may it miss you when it comes.

If you marry, may you marry last year.

That you may never see a bad day, and
if it sees you, may it be wearing glasses.

Good luck to you; your blood is worth bottling, and
may glass splinters blind hell's stokers.

May the wind be always at your back,
especially coming home on Saturday night.

A thousand blessings, maybe more,
Come down on you, *mo grádh, mo stór*;
Especially if you give your hand
To tend me and my plot of land.

Ireland is rearing them yet, and when
she's done may you wed the best of them.

May you live to be a hundred years and one extra year to atone.

Saints of glory protect us,
Holy Angels from the throne of God, guide us,
And if the devil still gets within a stone's throw of us,
May there be nothing but sand to *peg* (throw) at us.

May you never stay seeing the
bees without spotting the honey.

Bless the man who ploughs the furrow;
Ferrets rabbits from a burrow.
Bless his wife, may she not often
Ferret his last penny off him.

That you may have the appetite
of a horse; that's better than
having too much to eat!

May you be as well as you can bear to be.

May the hand that offers trouble
be as idle as the left hand of a bodhran.

May your horse always stand in the middle of the fair.

That your patch of trouble may not cover
the hole in a leprechaun's breeches.

May you get what you're after with
the help of God and two policemen.

Bless the horse that farts at noon,
Twice bless the one that farts at eve,
And thrice bless the work that makes him fart.

Toasts & Hearty Wishes

Whiskey, you're the devil,
You're leading me astray;
Over hills and mountains,
And to Americay.
You're sweeter, stronger, dacenter;
You're spunkier nor tay.
Oh whiskey, you're me darlin' drunk or sober!

Here's health and prosperity,
To you and all your posterity,
And them that doesn't drink with sincerity
That they may be damned for all eternity.

Good health to your enemies' enemies.

Hold your hour and have another!

Wet your whistle well and may
we never die of the drought!

Have another drink and may St. Peter think it's tay (*tea*)!

Health to you and yours; to mine and ours.
If mine and ours ever come across you and yours,
I hope that you and yours will do as much for mine and ours
As mine and ours have done for you and yours.

Whiskey is the life of man, whiskey Johnny!
Whiskey in an old tin can, whiskey for my Johnny.
(Belfast docks toast.)

Health and long life to you.
Land without rent to you.
A child every year to you,
And may you die in Ireland.

Good health without a cold in your pipes!

Here's to the first drop—the one that destroys you;
there's no harm at all in the last!

Here's one for the road, and may you know every turning!

Here's to the hand that made the ball,
That shot Lord Leitrim in Donegal.
(A Donegal toast.)

May the roof above us never fall in,
And may us good companions beneath it
Never fall out.

Thirst begets thirst,
So be getting yours first;
Good luck! Stay sane!
Down the dusty lane!

May the next drop make the grass grow
long on the road to hell for you!

Ireland's health and County Mayo,
And when that is lost, may we be alive;
The health of the hag from County Meath
And not out of love for her but her drop,
Your health from wall to wall
And the one outside the closed door, speak!

Here's to the same again or
something similar!

Sláinte! And when the world's troubles
are displayed on the floor, may you select your own.

When, from heaven God looks down
On your very last half-crown,
By a miracle, may it suddenly clink
'Gainst another one and ten,
Against twenty, twice again—
Just as long as you keep paying for the drink!

I drink the health of often-who-came,
Who often-comes-not I also must name;
'Though often-comes-not I must also blame,
For he comes not as often as often-who-came.

Saint Patrick was a gentleman;
Through strategy and strength
He drove the snakes from Erin.
A toast, then, to his health.
But not too many toasts, now,
Or you'll lose your sense and then
Forget about Saint Patrick
And meet all those snakes again.

May God never knock you down as long as
you keep putting them up!

So, all true blues, come fill your glass,
A better toast will never pass;
We'll drink unto the lovely lass,
The Orange Maid of Sligo.
(From "The Orange Maid of Sligo," nineteenth century ballad.)

Drink as if it was your last one
but may the last one not come till morning.

Seo sláinte mhinic-a-thig,
Agus seo sláinte minic-nach-dtig.
Is trua nach dtig minic-nach-dtig,
Leath chomh minic le minic-a-thig
(Health too often comes,
And health too seldom comes.
A pity that seldom comes
Does not come half as often as often comes.)

May God hold you in the hollow of his hand
and have a drink in the other for you.

At the end of the day,
Let us drink to work well done,
And if you are an idler,
We'll toast tomorrow's fun.

General Curses

Animals

A fox on your fishing hook.

May all the goats in Gorey chase you to hell.

May you buy every hair in your cow's tail.
(May you pay dearly for stock.)

May you find the bees but miss the honey.

That you may ever be a mile from
a cow's track—and the Lord doesn't
cross fields.

Curse of the crows on you.

The plight of the boiled and broken minnow to you.

A magpie on your wheat field gate.

May the man who would curse
the bladder out of a goat have a chat
with you before Christmas.

May the back of you get a salmon's roasting.
If ever you're on the pig's back,
I hope it's heading for the curing house.

May your horse have a sagging nosebag.

That your cat may bury you with its clap.

The curse of the goose that lost the quill that
wrote the Ten Commandments on you.

DEATH

That your bread may be baked.
(That you may die.)

For many a day may you rest in the clay.

Six horse loads of burial clay on you.

May there be red ribbons at your funeral.
(Red ribbons were once worn at the funeral of a murder victim.)

May they sing Eileen Aroon at your wake.
(Considered an unlucky song.)

May there never be enough of your people in heaven
to make a half-set.

May the company at your wake pray on cold flags.
(You will not get many prayers said for you.)

May you rot in the pauper's plot.

Hungry grass grow around your grave.
*(By custom, nobody would walk on it,
therefore no prayers would be said.)*

May you die without a priest in a town with no clergy.

May the foam of the river settle on you.
(May you drown.)

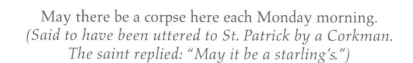

May there be a corpse here each Monday morning.
(Said to have been uttered to St. Patrick by a Corkman.
The saint replied: "May it be a starling's.")

May the only tears at your graveside be the onion-puller's.

Health & Wealth

May you have a little skillet,
May you have little in it.
May you have to break it
To find the little bit in it.

The consumption on you.

May your spuds be like rosary beads on the stalk.

At the going down of the sun may you have nothing
in your bag and less in your pocket.

That your pocket may drag your face into tripping you up.
(That your wealth may bring you unhappiness.)

May you someday follow the crow for your supper
and get bitten by a jackdaw.

The hand of God fall on you and your money.

May your trouble be in your throat.

May you never see the light of heaven
till you pay me what you owe me.

May you live to see the two days.
(Said to a wealthy person, wishing poverty.)

Hell & the Devil

May the devil behead all landlords
and make a day's work of their necks.

May you dance with a devil on your back.

May the devil weave your shroud
and may he pin the seams together.
*(A double curse, since using pins
in a shroud was considered unlucky.)*

The devil swallow you sideways.

The old boy settle your hash for you
and have your guts for garters.

When the bottom falls out of purgatory,
may you join the poor papists in hell.

Hell's hottest corner for you.

The devil set a place for you in hot contrary corner.

I'd ask Old Nick to make drisheens (*black pudding*) out of you,
only your blood is too watery.

Well I hope that Old Nick
Pokes your eyes with his stick,
Cuts your nose with a shears,
And burns off your big ears.

The devil shake you by the heels.

The devil's flame on you.

May the keystone of heaven's arch fall on you
and push you down below.

I'll carry you to the devil and may he take you out of my sight.

ILL LUCK

Ill luck to your mother for bearing you.

May you go stone blind so that
you won't know your wife from a headstone.
(John M. Feehan)

May there be guinea fowl crying at your child's birth.
(A bad luck sign.)

A taut, swift, suitable gallows-rope
Around the narrow, scrawny neck of the hanging scoundrel.

May you break your kneecap going down
the steep steps of your rosiest garden.

May the bard's curse on the man
who stole his harp fall on you.

Cold days and nights without a fire to you.

That you may meet your fetch at evening.
(Believed to bring bad luck.)

MISCELLANEOUS

A high windy gallows to you.
By the sod you stand on, curse not
You tread it but for a short while
But lie beneath it for eternity.

The madness of the brain on him,
A broken heart in him,
A heart-scourge beside him,
A hangman's noose around him.

O wretch of the crooked foot,
the crippled knee, and the squinting eye,
a thousand curses on you,
torn clothes on your back
and a pox on every bit of you.

O cursed hag who prays not to Mary,
may your teeth fall out
and may you disappear across the sea.

May I bend a coin on the Holy Ghost for you.
(Said as a sixpenny piece is hidden in a church to curse someone.)

Curse of the seven snotty orphans on you.

A red nail through the tongue that said it.

God's curse and his church's be on you.

The curse of the O'Flahertys on you.
*(The line of the powerful Galway clan was discontinued
because of a priest's curse.)*

Curse of the town on you.
(Uttered by a tinker who spent all his money carousing in a particular town.)

Curse of the wretched and the strong on the one who gave.

Bad luck to them that's *cloddin'* (throwing) stones

Your mouth and your face under you.
(Be "down in the mouth," therefore unhappy.)

He can quench the candle at the other side of the kitchen with a curse, and I hope he comes to your *céilí*.

May the gates of paradise never open to you.

The wretched state of the sinner and the gallows' knot to you.

God take the east and west from you—
The road before and behind you.

Three curses that cannot be countered:
The curse of a woman in labor,
The curse of a landless man,
The curse of a dead man.

Money & Poverty

The devil take your last shilling.

May you not have enough to buy your shroud.

May your Sunday best have its share of turtles
(threads hanging down).

May your thatch leak,
And your boots squeak.
May your eyes forever squint
And may you never have the *rint* (rent).

That you may have forty-five ways of putting
on your coat this harvest-time
(be in tatters).

May all belonging to you have to live on the smell of an oily rag.

That you may scratch a beggarman's back *(be a beggar yourself)*
some day.

Faith, may you follow the crow for that some day.
(Uttered when seeing some food thrown away.)

Faith, may you get your come uppance
before your pride wears down.

Curses from Poets & Writers

Lord, confound this surly sister,
Blight her brow with blotch and blister,
Cramp her larynx, lung, and liver,
In her guts a galling give her.
Let her live to earn her dinners
In Mountjoy with seedy sinners:
Lord, this judgement quickly bring,
And I'm your servant, J. M. Synge.
*(J. M. Synge, "The Curse." To a sister of an enemy of Synge's who
disapproved of his play,* The Playboy of the Western World.)

"Take our eyes, but leave us men,
Alive or dead,
Sons of Wattin!"
Sing the vengeance of the Welshmen of Tirawley.
(Samuel Ferguson, "The Forging of the Anchor.")

Grief on you, Morris!
Heart's blood and bowels' blood!
May your eyes go blind
And your knees be broken! ...
Destruction pursue you,
Morris the traitor,
Who brought death to my husband!
Father of three children
Two on the hearth
And one in the womb
That I will not bring forth.
(Eileen O'Connell,"The Lament for Art O'Leary.")

"Death to every foe and traitor! Forward! Strike the marching tune!"
(John Keegan Casey, "The Rising of the Moon.")

Woe is me! by fraud and wrong,
Traitors false and tyrants strong,
Fell Clan Usnach, bought and sold,
For Barach's feast and Conor's gold!

Woe to Eman, roof and wall!
Woe to Red Branch, hearth and hall!—
Tenfold woe and black dishonour
To the foul and false Clan Conor!
(Samuel Ferguson, "Deirdre's Lament for the Sons of Usnach.")

Searing mountains and scalding heart
Curse that place of drowning.
For its many the creature it has left in woe
Thinking and mourning each Monday morning.
(Antoine Ó Reachtabhra, "Anach Cúain.")

AMUSING IMPRECATIONS

May the man who steals my flute lose
the power of his limbs and never blow even soup.

That Cromwell's corpse may rise again
and give you good looks.

Forty weasels chew your lights,
Perforate your bowels with bites
Till you're leaking like a collander of gruel.
May a ferret with a grin
Lash its molars to your chin
As you scream in pain like Festy Flynn, the fool.

May you starve till you can kiss a goat between the horns.

May you croak, confound you, and may you get the pip
(a disease in fowl).

Six eggs to you and a half-dozen of them rotten.

May you suffer everything that Cromwell
might give except his money.
May you have nothing in your bag at the going
down of the sun and less when it rises.

That you may wear out more sheets than soles.
That the only full pockets you'll ever have be in your habit.

A curse on your house if you have one; if you haven't,
blast the stars.

That your feet may have blisters
when they're dancing the angel's hornpipe.

Well wear, soon tear,
Then you can give the ragman his share.

When the last train leaves for heaven may you still be in
the waiting room.

When it rains gold, may you be without a spoon.

Proverbs

lthough the following pieces of traditional advice—in the form of proverbs—were collected over sixty years ago, many are still used today. This is because proverbs survive over time if their message continues to be appropriate in the new era.

Most of the proverbs found in Ireland can also be found in various languages throughout many other countries of Europe. They can also be found in other continents where Europeans settled and so demonstrate cultural connections. As in other places, proverbs in Ireland can have a complex history and each would need to be studied individually to be certain of its journey between countries and languages.

The repertoire of proverbs used by any particular community reflects its concerns and values, and a great number of them draw their metaphors from everyday life. While the images in the proverbs draw largely on the local surroundings familiar to the proverb users—the bogs and the green fields and hills with their whins and briars—they also contain fascinating references to the wider world, and to exotica, such as silks, satins, and velvet.

Fireside & Candlelight

Keep your house and your house will keep you.

A house divided will soon fall.

There can be no window where there is no wall.

There is no hearthstone like your own hearthstone.

Bare walls make giddy housekeepers.

A red chimney, a hot house.

It is easier to build two chimneys than
to keep smoke in one.

It is easy to kindle a fire on an old hearth.
It is never hard to light a half-burned turf.
*(Turf or peat is the fossil fuel from a bog
and it was once extensively used.)*

A spark may raise an awful blaze.

Little sticks kindle a fire, great ones put it out.

A little fire to warm you is better than a great one to harm you.

Never burn a penny candle
looking for a halfpenny.

When the two ends are alight,
the candle does not burn long.

Sweep the corners—the middle will sweep itself.

A new broom sweeps clean but
the old one knows the corners best.

Ash green makes a fire for the queen.
*(Ash green would be fresh,
unseasoned ash wood.)*

You can't make a piano out of a bacon box.

Never bolt your door with a boiled carrot.

Many feathers make a bed.
*(A sack can be filled with
even small potatoes.)*

Food & Drink

"My belly thinks my throat is cut," the hungry man said.

A hungry eye sees far.
(The hungry person's eye is sharp.)

Hunger is a good sauce; if it doesn't choke you, it will fatten you.

Hunger will conquer a lion.

Talk doesn't fill the stomach.

As is the cook, so is the kitchen.

A blunt knife shows a bad housekeeper.

A good fire makes a speedy cook.

What won't choke will fatten and clean dirt is no poison.

Last one to the work, first one to the table.

Help is always welcome, except at the table.

It is easy to be *flaithiúil* (generous) with another person's share.

You don't know what is in the pot till the lid is lifted.

Cool before you sup.

A fat kitchen never leaves a lean will.

A fat kitchen makes a lean purse.

A full stomach never thinks of an empty one.

Scant feeding to man or horse is a small profit and sure loss.

He sups ill, who eats all at dinner.
*(Dinner is the meal at midday, which was usually
the most substantial one of the day.)*

One without dinner means two for supper.

BUTTER & BUTTER MAKING

A running cow's milk is hard to churn.

The longer the churning, the tougher the butter.

The more water, the less butter.

Yellow butter sells best.

Some people, when they get their heads
above the churn, would not drink buttermilk.
(Buttermilk means little to me when I am full of it.)

The person who has butter gets more butter.

Butter won't choke a cat.
*(There are many ways of choking
a cat besides choking it with butter.)*

Don't buy butter for cats to lick.

Butter to butter is no kitchen.
(Kitchen *is relish—a little dab of something well-flavored added to plain fare to make it more appetizing.*)

Champ to champ will choke you.
(Champ *is a name used in northern parts of the island for mashed potatoes.*)

Meal, Porridge & Bread

Always going to the chest and never putting in, soon brings the meal to the bottom.
(Meal *was often stored in a wooden chest.*)

There is skill in all things, even in making porridge.

Nature binds the meal to the potstick.

Where there's meal, there is surely salt.

Don't put in your spoon where there is no porridge.

Don't scald your lips with another man's porridge.

It is easy to bake beside the meal.

A man who has a loaf will get a knife to cut it.

A slice off half a loaf is not missed.

Crooked bread makes straight bellies.

Raw *dods* make fat lads.
(A dod is a lump of bread.)

Broth, Meat, Fish & Vegetables

You cannot sup soup with a fork.
(It is only nonsense to be drinking soup with a fork.)

The second boiled broth is always the best.

A stew boiled is a stew spoiled.

Keep your heart up for fretting is but
bad kitchen to your meat.
*(Keep your heart up, we will
have good weather yet.)*

A bit of a rabbit is worth two bits of a cat.

A pig's ear can never make mutton.

Don't pluck your goose until you catch her.
(Don't give thanks for your food until it is in your bag.)

The younger the chicken,
the sweeter the picking.

Chicken today and feathers tomorrow.

An egg today is better than
a roasted ox tomorrow.

Better is a small fish than an empty dish.
(One single potato is better than a plateful of skins.)

A good apple eater is a bad sharer.

Better have potatoes and salt—and peace.

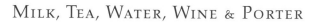

Milk, Tea, Water, Wine & Porter

The juice of a cow is good alive or dead.

No cure for spilled milk, only licking the pitcher.

Don't skim the top off the
milk before you send it
to the creamery.

Tea seldom spoils
when water boils.

There is nothing as mean
as tea in a tin.

He who only drinks water
does not get drunk.

Water is a good drink if taken in the right spirit.

Wine drowns more men than water.

Wine is sweet but the results are bitter.

The three faults of drink are:
a sorrowful morning,
a dirty coat,
and an empty pocket.

You'll never miss the water
till the well runs dry.

Empty kettles never leak.

Farm Animals

Donkeys & Horses

What would you expect from a donkey but a kick?

I cannot whistle, chew meal, and drive a donkey.
(It is not possible to be driving the cows and milking them.)

Better is a donkey that carries you than a horse that throws you.

A whip for the horse, a bridle for the donkey,
and a rod for the fool's back.

Better a poor horse in an empty stall;
better half a loaf than none at all.

Those who would slight my
horse would buy my horse.

You can't judge a horse by his harness.

He's a good horse that pulls his own load.

It is a proud horse won't carry his own corn.
(Corn *is the common name for oats.*)

An old horse needs fresh grass.

A borrowed horse has hard hooves, or has no soul.

Cows

"Every man to his fancy, and me to my own Nancy,"
said the old woman when she kissed her cow.

The worst cow in the barn bawls first.
The cow with the dirtiest tail lows loudest.

The taste of the clover makes a thief of the cow.

The old cow for the sour grass.
(Sour grass *is coarse grass.*)

From her head the cow is milked.

A starved cow never fills the pail.

I'd far rather the cow that would give the full
of a thimble than the one that would give
the full of a churn and spill it.
Better a goat that only gives a
thimbleful of milk than a cow that
gives a churnful and spills it.

What is the use of a good cow when she spills her milk?

A bad cow is better than none.

SHEEP & GOATS

Tethered sheep will not thrive.

Do not lose the sheep for a halfpenny worth of tar.

Every scabby sheep likes a comrade.

There never was a scabby sheep in the flock
that did not like to have a companion with her.

One scabby sheep spoils a whole flock.

If one sheep puts his head through the gap,
the rest will follow.

When you see a goat,
you should always hit him
because he is either going into
mischief or coming out of it.

When the goat goes to the door of the chapel,
she will not stop until she goes to the altar.

If you put a silk suit on a goat, it is still a goat.

It is difficult to cut wool off a goat.

Riding on a goat is better than
the best of walking.

Dogs & Cats

What could you expect from a dog but a bite?

Idle dogs worry sheep.

A well-bred dog goes out when he sees
them preparing to kick him out.

A dog with two homes is never any good.

Don't let your bone go with the dog.

Keep the bone and the dog will follow.

The dog that fetches will carry.

Every dog has his day and some have two.

An old dog cannot alter his way of barking.

To steal an old dog, never try;
you'll find your mistake by and by.

It's hard to teach an old dog to dance.

You should not throw stones at a dead dog.

If the cat was churning, it was often
she would have her paws in it.

A wise cat never burned herself.

Too many cats are worse than rats.

If the cat sits long enough at the hole,
she will catch the mouse.

A cat purrs for itself.

Nature shines through the cat's eyes.

What's in the cat is in the kitten.

HENS, GEESE & DUCKS

It is a bad hen that can't scrape for herself.

A laying hen is better than a nest of eggs.

The sitting hen never fattens.

You can't expect a big egg from a little hen.

It is not the hen that cackles most that
lays the largest egg.

Cultivation

He takes the shortcut to food but the long way to work.

The man that waits for a good day will get it.

A farmer's work is never done.

From the king to the beggar,
they all depend on the farmer.

He who is a bad servant for himself is often
a good servant for others.

Work is better than talk.

Work while the bit is in your belly.

The more you tramp the dunghill, the more the dirt rises.

The grass-harrow gathers no stones.

You should never stop the plough to kill a mouse.

Seed must be saved before it's sown.

If you don't sow in the spring, you
will not reap in the autumn.

The seed you will sow is the corn you will reap.

More grows in a tilled field than is sowed in it.

Time will tell and frost will dry the praties.
(Praties *is a colloquial word for potatoes.)*

A good farmer is known by his crops.

It is not the big farmers who reap all the harvest.

"Time enough" never cut the barley.

APPLES & ORCHARDS

No use in throwing apples into an orchard.

Many a rose-cheeked apple is rotten at the core.

The shakiest tree in the orchard
is sometimes the last to fall.

Little apples will grow big.
(Big potatoes develop from little potatoes.)

When the apple is ripe, it will fall.

Don't wait for apples; gather your own windfalls.

The tree remains but not so the hand that put it.

Hunting & Fishing

A flying bird is any person's shot.

The wise bird flies lowest.

A closed fist never caught a bird.

An old fox is shy of a trap.

An old rogue is a good tracker.

It is hard to hunt the hare out of the bush it is not in.

Nearly never killed the hare.

Long runs the hare but she is caught at last.

Don't make bold with the sea.

Listen to the sound of the river and you will catch a trout.

When you're not fishing, be mending the nets.

It's late to be mending your nets when the eels are in the river.
(It's late to throw out the anchor when the ship is on the rock.)

A trout in the ashes is better than a salmon in the water.

Woods & Wells

Never be first in the bog or last in the wood.

If there is a way into the wood, there is also a way out of it.

Don't crow till you're out of the woods.

Bend with the tree that will bend with you.

If the rowan tree is tall, even so, it is bitter on top.

An apple can't grow on a crab tree.

The older the crab tree, the more crabs it bears.

Willows are weak, but they bind other wood.

The deeper the well, the better the water.

It's a pure spring that never runs dry.

If you break the ice, it is easy lifting a bucket of water.

Wildlife

A sleeping fox catches no fowl.

The fox never found a better messenger than itself.

The fox finds its own stink first.

The last kick of a dying rat is always the worst.

Little by little, the bird builds its nest.

You can't teach a swallow how to fly.

A sand lark can't attend two strands.

A wild goose never lays a tame egg.

A swan would die with pride
only for its black feet.

Every little frog is great in its own bog.

HIGH ROADS & BYROADS

Never cross the fields while you have the road to go.
(Do not abandon the main road for the sake of a shortcut.)

Be the road straight or crooked, the high road is the shortest.

First-class walking is better than third-class riding.

A stirring foot always gets something, even if it's only a thorn.

The loosest spoke in the wheel rattles most.

An empty cart makes the most noise.

A car on the road earns money,
but two in the ditch earns nothing.

Short answers fit travelers.

A rolling stone gathers no moss, but it gets a great shine.

The longest road has an end and the straightest road has an end.

The way to a friend's house is never long.

Two shorten the road.

It is a long road that has no public house!

Money & Markets

It is a poor village that has neither smoke nor fire.

There's always money where there's dirt.

Money is like muck—no good till spread.

If you don't speculate, you won't accumulate.

Money would make the pot boil
if you would throw ice in the fire.

A penny in a poor man's pocket is better
than two pennies in a rich man's pocket.

You may not be talking of a penny
when you have not a halfpenny.

Your eye is your mark, your pocket is your friend;
let the money be the last thing you'll part with.

Never buy through your ears but through your eyes.

Taste and try before you buy.

Don't bring all your eggs to one market.

If you have only a buck goat,
be in the middle of the fair with him.

No cow, no care, no errand to the fair.

The Law

Don't go to law with the devil in the court of hell.

If you go to court, leave your soul at home.

Circumstances alter cases, broken noses alter faces.

A word in the court is worth a pound in the purse.

A good friend in court is better than money in the purse.

A pennyworth of law is enough for anyone.

Law is costly; shake hands and be friends.

Lawyers' houses are made of fools' heads.

A lawmaker is a lawbreaker.

The law is no respecter of persons.

Friends & Neighbors

A man is known by his company.

As you live yourself, you judge your neighbor.

There is more friendship in a half of whiskey
than in a churn of buttermilk.

Friends are like fiddle strings
and they must not be screwed too tightly.

Don't be hard and don't be soft,
and don't desert your friend for your own share.

It is a pity on a man that is content
in the troubles of his neighbors.

Don't outstay your welcome like a neighbor's goat.

Come seldom, come welcome.
Go only seldom to your friend's house
and you will be welcomed.

Everyone is nice till the cow
gets into the garden.

Good mearings make
good neighbors.
(Mearing *is a boundary
between land owned
by different people.*)

Everybody is sweet to your face until you
burn a stack of turf with them.

You have your neighbor when your friends are far away.
If you have not your neighbor, you have nobody.

Don't take a slate off your own
house to put on your neighbor's.

The war of friends doesn't last long.

Occupations

One that has a trade has an estate.

A good tradesman has all his tools.

Though the carpenter is bad, the splinter is good.

Old masons make good barrowmen.

A bad cobbler will never make a shoemaker.

If you knew everything, you could be a doctor.

Charity covers a multitude of sins,
but a tailor covers a multitude of sinners.

Never judge cloth by tailors' words.

If *ifs* and *ands* were pots and pans,
there would be no need for tinsmiths' hands.

A tinker's wife and a tailor's wife are
the two that never agree.

Clothes & Appearance

Beauty is only skin deep;
ugliness goes to the bone.

Beauty never boiled the pot and ugliness never thickened it.

An inch is a great deal on a nose.

Many an honest heart beats under a ragged coat.

Stitch by stitch the suit is made.

Patch beside patch is neighborly,
but patch upon patch is beggarly.

You cannot tell from a man's clothes
how much he is making,
but you must look at his wife's.

Fancy buys the ribbon but taste ties the bow.

Charity covers a multitude of sins
and an overcoat covers a multitude of rags.

You cannot take a glove off the hand that it is not on.

God's leather to God's weather.

The beauty of an old shoe is to polish it.

Bad shoes are better than none.

Never throw away the old boots till you get new ones.

Many a white collar covers a dirty neck.

Any fool carries an umbrella on a wet day
but the wise man carries it every day.

Health

A glutton lives to eat, a wise man eats to live.

Diet cures more than the doctor.

Better to pay the cook than the doctor.

Sleep is better than medicine.

A good laugh and a long sleep are
the two best cures in the doctor's book.

A good laugh is as good as a day at the seaside.

A day in the country is worth a month in the town.

What butter or whiskey will not cure is incurable.

Whiskey when you're sick makes you well;
whiskey makes you sick when you're well.

A light heart lives long.

A heavy heart seldom combs a gray head.

Three places to be avoided:
a doctor's door, a priest's door, and a barrack door.

DEATH

You're late to run for the priest
when the person is dead.

Deaths and marriages make changes.

Death takes the young as well as the old.

Death never gives a year's
warning to anyone.

Death comes like a thief in the night.

There is hope from the sea
but no hope from the cemetery.

What you think is worse than
your death is perhaps for your good.

A wise man never saw a dead man.

It is easy to rob a dead man's house.

LUCK

Luck's a king and luck's a beggar.

Luck and laziness go hand in hand.

Good luck beats early rising.

Better to be fortunate than rich.

It is better to be lucky than wise.

There is no luck where there is no correction.

Bad luck never comes alone.

Good care takes the head off bad luck.

The worse luck now the better again later.

When luck comes, it comes in a bucketful.

Irish Folk Wisdom

The Animal Kingdom

Calves

Be it fat or lean, pity the man that
won't rear a calf for himself.

Grass that hasn't grown will suit the unborn calf.

One calf is better than two skins.

Many things befall the calf that his dam never thought of.

The calf's skin often goes to market before his mother's.

Smooth is the calf that his mother licks.

Cats

What can you expect from a cat but her skin?

If the cat had a churn, her paw would often be in it.

What would a young cat do but kill a mouse?

A man who is idle will put the cat on the fire.

The cat's milk makes no cream.

Cats never do good but in spite of themselves.

It's not good to be telling lies,
as the cat said when the wolf ate him.

The cat's leavings are fit only for himself.

It's not easy to put pants on a cat.

If the cat sits long enough at the hole,
she will catch the mouse.

Who knows best to take the cat out of the churn
but he that put her in?

Combat the cat and it will bristle up.

Every cat is gray at night.

The cats would do well till the mice
would take their ears off.

The cat may look at the king,
but the king may put the eyes out of the cat.

The cat wonders at its having a tail.

Cows

Out of her head the cow is milked.

Far-off cows have long horns.

Show the fatted calf
but not the thing that fattened him.

In winter the milk goes to the cow's horns.

A bad cow is better than none.

Shun a cow's horn and a horse's hinder parts.

One cow breaks the fence and a dozen leap it.

Cows wear with milking.

A cow is only a good deal bigger than the midge.

You can't sell the cow and drink her milk.

All the cows do not come equally to the fold.

I'd rather have the cow that would fill a thimble
than one that would fill a churn and spill it.

The low is greater than the milking.

Better have no cow than no son.

A starved cow never fills the pail.

The cow is the first to notice her own calf.

Deer

Food will tame the mountain deer.

The swiftness of the roe is known
without the loosing of the hounds.

The fawn is swifter than its mother.

The older the buck, the harder his horn.

Don't skin the deer till you get it.

Dogs

Hit a dog with a bone and it won't growl.

Quarrelsome dogs get dirty coats.

The hungry hound thinks not of its whelps.

One dog will cause all the others to bark.

Be good to the dog and it will follow you.

The moon is none the worse of the dogs barking at it.

There is no fight like the old dog's fight.

There never was a swift dog that didn't get its fill of work.

An old dog cannot change its way of barking.

A dog may have a spirit as well as a man.

A dog's grin is just like an Englishman's laugh.

One dog fleeing is swifter than twelve pursuing.

A bad name kills dogs.

The more a dog gets, the more it wants.

A house without a dog is a house without laughter.

Playing with a pup ends in a howl.

A dog is the better off for another dog being reproved.

It's an ill dog that is not worth the whistling.

A slow hound is often lucky.

Foxes

The fox never found a better messenger than itself.

The fox will go no farther than its feet will carry him.

He who would cheat the fox must rue early.

If the fox runs into the hound's embrace, who's to blame?

In spite of the fox's cunning, its skin is often sold.

GOATS

It's no use going to the goat's house to look for wool.

Do not mistake a goat's beard for a fine stallion's tail.

If you see a goat, hit it because it's either getting into mischief or just getting out of it.

It is natural for the kid to bleat.

The kid will soon be worse than the old buck.

The goats will be deaf at harvest time.

HORSES

Many a shabby colt makes a fine horse.

It's easy to see a white horse in a bog.

Everyone lays a burden on the willing horse.

Even a good horse cannot keep running forever.

A nod is as good as a wink to a blind horse.

He that buys an old hack will have to buy another horse.

When you mount your high horse, you tumble over it.

It's hard to stop an old horse from kicking.

It is no shame to a person to be thrown by a mare.

An old horse needs fresh grass.

Though the man is the farmer,
the horse is the laborer.

An inch of a horse is better than a foot of a mare.

A good horse may be forgiven a kick.

Often it's not the best horse that wins the race.

PIGS

The miller's pigs are fat,
but God knows whose meal they ate.

A person that's made a pet of and a pig that's made a pet of
are the two worst pets of all.

Pigs won't thrive on clean water.

It's not the pick of the swine that the beggar gets.

From the sow comes but a little pig.

It's not the big sow that eats the most.

It's on the fat pig the butter goes.

As a jewel in a pig's snout is a woman
without understanding.

A thieving pig's ear can hear the grass growing.

SHEEP

There was never a scabby sheep in a
flock that didn't like to have a comrade.

You might as well hang for a sheep as for a goat.

In spring when the sheep is lean, shellfish are fat.

A white sheep may have a black lamb,
and a black sheep a white one.

The ragged sheep that goes into the briars
will leave her wool there.

Tethered sheep will not thrive.

If the briar were not in the way, the sheep would not go into it.

A lamb when carried far becomes as burdensome as a sheep.

BIRDS

The silly bird's foot will go into the snare.

Birds do not light on only one branch.

Where the fish is, there the birds will be.

Though the egg be small,
a bird will come out of it.

Sweet sings each bird in its own grove.

The hungry bird fights best.

The birds are good in their native place.

CHICKENS

As the old rooster crows, so the young bird chirrups.

Loud cackle, little egg.

A laying hen is better than a nest of eggs.

A black hen will lay a white egg.

The hen is very bountiful with the horse's corn.

It's a bad hen that can't scratch for herself.

You can't expect a big egg from a little hen.

The sitting hen never fattens.

CROWS

Wherever the crow goes it'll take its tail with it.

It is in the evening the crow makes water.

A crow won't caw without a reason.

GEESE

Even the geese understand each other.

Don't pluck your goose until you catch it.

A wild goose never laid a tame egg.

Those who have a goose will get a goose.

WRENS

The wren spreads its feet wide in its own home.

"'Tis the less for that, 'tis the less for that,"
as the wren said when it sipped a billful out of the sea.
"It's the bigger of that, it's the bigger of that,"
as the wren said when it pissed in the sea.

A wren in the hand is better than a crane to be caught.

Although the wren is small, it will make a noise.

FISH

The fish that bites every worm will be caught in time.

Dry shoes won't get fish.

There are finer fish in the sea than have ever been caught.

Where the fish is, the birds will be.

A little fish is better than no fish at all.

Do not bless the fish until it is landed.

INSECTS & REPTILES

An ant has only to look on an eagle to know its own insignificance.

A fly is of little account until it gets into the eye.

When a sharp point pierces the frog, it shrieks.

You can't pluck a frog.

'Tis not where water is, a frog will be,
but where a frog is, water will be.

Love & Marriage

Love

What is nearest the heart is nearest the lips.

Live in my heart and pay no rent.

I love you—and what you have.

They won't fall in love with the man they don't see.

Constant gazing betokens love.

Love is blind to blemishes and fault.

Love a dunghill and you'll see no motes in it.

When the sight leaves the eye, love leaves the heart.

After the dowry comes the love.

She who fills the heart
fills the eye.

Love is no impartial judge.

Love conceals ugliness,
and hate sees many faults.

MARRIAGE

Woe to him who does not heed a good wife's counsel.

Marriages are all happy; it's having breakfast together
that causes all the problems.

Young man, you'll be troubled till you marry,
and from then on you'll never have rest.

A growing moon and a flowing tide are lucky times to marry.

There are no trials until one gets married.

A ring on the finger and not a stitch of clothes on the back.

The blanket is the warmer for being doubled.

He married money and got a woman with it.

There's no feast until a roast and no torment until a marriage.

Better a wise wife than a plow and land.

There'll be white blackbirds before an unwilling woman marries.

Take no woman for a wife who presents herself without a flaw.

The day you marry your wife you marry your children.

Do not take a wife from a mansion or a cow from a gardener.

I married a trollop for her gear;
her gear is gone, but she's still here.

Marriage will sober love.

Children

A son like the mother
and a daughter like the father.

Praise the child and it will progress.

The unfortunate only son naturally goes to the dogs.

If children won't make you laugh,
they won't make you cry.

The child that's left to himself will
put his mother to shame.

Baptize your own child first.

A child will be known by its manners.

A woman may bear a son, but God makes the heir.

What the child sees is what the child does.

The feeding of a growing boy would a grain mill aye employ.

Every finger has not the same length,
nor every son the same disposition.

Your son is your son today,
but your daughter is your daughter forever.

Every mother thinks it's
for her own child the sun rises.

No man ever wore a tie as nice as
his child's arm around his neck.

There's no love until there's a family.

HOUSE & HEARTH,
FOOD & DRINK

HOUSE & HEARTH

Wide is the door of the little cottage.

A hut is a palace to a poor man.

The eye should be blind in the house of another.

A little fire that warms is better than a big fire that burns.

Firelight will not let you read fine stories,
but it's warm and you won't see the dust on the floor.

The old pipe gives the sweetest smoke.

Silk and satin and scarlet leave a fireless, colorless hearth.

Even a tin knocker will shine on a dirty door.

A windy day is not the day for thatching.

It is easier to demolish a house than to build one.

Food

Hunger is a good sauce.

Good humor comes from the kitchen.

You don't know what's in the pot until the lid is lifted.

No fumes from the pot, but from what it contains.

All living creatures must be fed.

'Tis pleasant with company at the table;
woe to him who eats alone.

Help is a good thing except at the dinner table.

Food is a workhorse.

Though honey is sweet, do not lick it off a briar.

No feast till there is the roast.

Where there's meal, there's bound to be salt.

Never scald your lips on another man's porridge.

You look for the ladle when the pot's on the fire.

Let broth boil slowly, but let porridge make a noise.

You must crack the nut before you can eat the kernel.

He is like the bagpipes;
he never makes a noise till his belly's full.

DRINK

He who drinks only water never gets drunk.

Wine is old men's milk.

Sweet is the wine but sour's the payment.

What butter and whiskey won't cure, there's no cure for.

It's the first drop that destroyed me;
there's no harm at all in the last.

A drink is shorter than a story.

Do not be talkative in an alehouse.

Drunkenness and anger speak truth.

Choose your company before you drink.

You take your health once too often
to the whiskey shop till it gets broken.

It's sweet to drink but bitter to pay for it.

Thirst after the drink and sorrow after the money.

When good luck comes, the drink comes.

Thirst begets thirst.

Drunkenness will not protect a secret.

The end of drinking is more thirst.

The cure of the drinking is to drink again.

The inebriated heart will not lie.

Wine is the best liquor to wash glasses in.

God & The Devil

God

God's help is nearer than the door.

When God comes in the door,
the devil flies out the window.

God is not as severe as he is said to be.

God fits the back to suit the burden.

God often pays debts without money.

God is good till morning.

God moves slowly, yet his grace comes.

God shares the good things.

God never closes one door without opening another.

The love of God guides every good.

Whatever God has given me, I cannot sell.

Man talks but God directs.

The Devil

It's easy to preach to the devil with a full stomach.

Never bid the devil good morrow until you meet him.

Speak to the devil and you'll hear the thunder of his hooves.

The man of horns is active.

To praise God is proper,
but a wise person won't blackguard the devil.

Better is the devil you know than the devil you don't know.

The devil dances in an empty pocket.

The devil wipes his tail with the poor man's pride.

The devil never took a
good heart to hell.

YOUTH & AGE

Young people don't know what age is,
and old people forget what youth was.

It's difficult to put an old head on a
young shoulder.

Bend the sapling while it is young.

Praise the young and they will make progress.

Youth likes to wander.

Make your hay before the fine weather leaves you.

To be old and decayed dishonors no one.

Honor belongs to old age.

When the twig hardens, it is difficult to twist it.

Good sense comes only with age.

The older the fiddle, the sweeter the tune.

RICH & POOR

Sweet is the voice of the person who has wealth.

A shamefaced person seldom acquires wealth.

The doorstep of a great house is slippery.

A heavy purse makes a light heart.

The more you get, the less you have.

Better be bordering on plenty
than be in the very middle of poverty.

Though you love your wealth, keep your good name;
for if you lose that, you are worthless.

The person whose stomach is well-filled
does not understand the needs of the hungry.

Poverty is no shame, but shame is ever a part of poverty.

It's no use carrying an umbrella if your shoes are leaking.

If you must be in rags,
let your rags be tidy.

Those who have not meat
find soup a luxury.

No one is ever poor who has the sight of their eyes
and the use of their feet.

Though high above the poor the rich may look,
they will be all together yet.

Friends & Neighbors

Prove a friend before you need him.

Tell me who your friends are and I'll tell you who you are.

Friends are better than gold.

Take care but take no sides,
and on no account sacrifice your friends.

Pick your company before you sit down.

The friend that can be bought is not worth buying.

Friendship is good though separation is painful.

Reverence ceases once blood is spilled.

Don't show your skin to the person who won't cover it.

The coldness of a friend,
like the coldness of linen,
never lasts long.

Better a little of one's own
than many friends.

The coldness of a friend is better than the sweetness
of an enemy.

If you will walk with lame men and woman,
you will soon limp yourself.

The person long absent is forgotten.

A friend's eye is a good looking glass.

WISE MAN & FOOL

There are two things that can't be cured—death and stupidity.

Everyone is wise until they speak.

Though wisdom is good in the beginning,
it is better at the end.

A wise person will form a year's judgment
from one night's knowledge of another person.

A little of anything isn't worth a bean,
but a little bit of sense is worth a lot.

Gold is light with a fool.

There's never been a wise person without a fault.

The person with least knowledge talks most.

Food is no more important than wisdom.

The fool may pass for wise if he holds his tongue.

Anger may look in on a wise person's heart,
but it abides in the heart of a fool.

Don't give cherries to pigs;
don't give advice to fools.

No fools are so intolerable
as those who affect to be wits.

Wisdom is what makes a poor man a king,
a weak person powerful,
a good generation of a bad one,
and a foolish man reasonable.

He's a fool who'll not take advice,
but he's a thousand times worse who takes every advice.

Toil & Labor

The sweat of one's brow is what burns everyone.

If he's not fishing, he's mending his nets.

There's no need to fear the wind if your haystacks are tied down.

The seeking for one thing will find another.

If the knitter is weary, the baby will have no new bonnet.

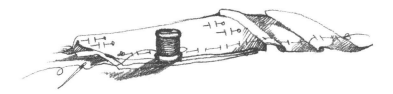

You'll never plow a field by turning it over in your mind.

A person may force a livelihood,
but they cannot force fortune.

Better not to begin than to stop without finishing.

Night is a good shepherd: It brings home man and beast.

The dog that's always on the go is better than
the one that's always curled up.

A little man can take his share from
the land when a tall man cannot take his from the sky.

Feeding the land before it gets hungry,
giving it rest before it gets weary,
and weeding it well before it gets dirty
are the marks of a good farmer.

Better a handful of craftsmanship
than a handful of gold.

Better the diligence of the weak person
than the indifference of a strong person.

The person of the greatest talk is the person of the least work.

Better small corn seeds out of bad land than no seed at all.

Fat is not to be had without labor.

Speed and accuracy do not agree.

TRIADS

Three things that cannot be acquired—a voice,
generosity, and poetry.

Three things that are never seen—a blade's edge,
wind, and love.

The three things most difficult to go through—a waterfall,
a bog, and a briary path.

The three happiest creatures in the world—the tailor,
the piper, and the goat.

Three signs of the lucky person—diligence,
early rising, and good fences.

The three sweetest melodies—
the churning of butter,
the plow plowing, and the mill grinding.

Three signs of the unlucky individual—long visits to neighbors,
long morning sleep, and bad fences.

Three things that arrive unnoticed—rent, age, and a beard.

Three things that stay longest in a family—fighting,
thieving, and red hair.

Three things to have in abundance—sunshine,
wisdom, and generosity.

The three worst endings—a house burning, a ship sinking,
and an old white horse dying.

Three things that relate to drink—to carry it,
to pay for it, and to consume it.

Three kinds of brains—brains as hard as stone, brains as receptive as wax, and brains as unstable as flowing water.

Three good things to have—a clean shirt, a clean conscience, and a guinea in the pocket.

Words To The Wise

Humor is like a feather pillow—it is filled with what is easy to get, but gives great comfort.

It's hard to fight with the wide ocean.

A word goes to the winds, but a blow goes to the bones.

The best way to keep loyalty in a person's heart is to keep money in their pocket.

Every foot is slow on an unknown path.

When angry words arise, a closed mouth is soothing.

The longest road out is the shortest road home.

A patch is better than a hole,
but a hole is more
honorable than a patch.

A scholar's ink lasts longer than a martyr's blood.

Never run after a bus or a woman.
There will always be another
one along in a few minutes.

Face the sun but turn your back to the storm.

Say but little and say it well.

To know a person one must live
in the same house with him.

If it's worth taking, it's worth asking for.

There is no cure for grief but to put it underfoot.

Do not light a fire you cannot yourself put out.

Irish Cures, Mystic Charms & Superstitions

ANCIENT CURES

ll nations and races from the earliest time have held the intuitive belief that mystic beings were always around them, influencing, though unseen, every action of life and all the forces of nature. They felt the presence of a spirit in the winds, and the waves, and the swaying branches of the forest trees, and in the primal elements of all that exists. Fire was to them the sacred symbol of the divine essence, ever striking toward ascension; and water, ever seeking a level, was the emblem of the purification that should cover all daily life; while in the elemental earth, they reverenced the power that produces all things, and where all that lives finds a grave, yet also a resurrection.

Thus, to the primitive races of humankind, the unseen world of mystery was a vital and vivid reality; the great oversoul of the visible, holding a mystic and psychic relation to humanity, and ruling it through the instrumentality of beings who had a strange power either for good or evil over human lives and actions.

We turn back the leaves of the national legends of all countries and peoples, and find stamped on the first page the words "God and Immortality." These two ideas are at the base of all the old-world thought and culture and underlie all myths, rituals, and monuments, and all the antique usages and mystic lore of charms, incantations, and sacrificial observances.

The Irish Doctors

From the most ancient pagan times, the Irish doctors were renowned for their skill in the treatment of disease, and the professors of medicine held a high and influential position in the druid order. They were allowed a distinguished place at the royal table, next to the nobles and above the armorers, smiths, and workers in metals; they were also entitled to wear a special robe of honor when at the courts of the kings and were always attended by a large staff of pupils, who assisted the master in the diagnosis and treatment of disease and the preparations necessary for the curative potions.

The skill of the Irish physicians was based chiefly upon a profound knowledge of the healing nature and properties of herbs; and they were also well acquainted with the most deadly and concentrated poisons that can be found in the common field plants.

But, in addition to the aid given by science and observation, they also practiced magic with great effect, knowing well how strongly charms, incantations, and fairy cures can act on the nerves and impress the mind of a patient. Consequently, their treatment of disease was of a medical-religious character, in which various magic ceremonials largely helped the curative process.

For Ague

A few spiders tied up in a bag and worn round the neck will keep off fever and ague; but none, save the fairy doctor, must ever open the bag to look at the contents, or the charm will be broken.

For ague, a small living spider should be rolled up in a cobweb, then put into a lump of butter and eaten while the fit is on. Pills also may be made of the cobwebs in which the eggs remain and taken daily for three days after which time it would be dangerous to continue the treatment.

For Apoplexy

A spoonful of aqua vitae sweetened with sugar, and a little grated bread added that it may not annoy the brain or the liver, will preserve from lethargy and apoplexy and all cold diseases.

For Asthma

Let the patient drink of a potion made of dandelion (*dent de lion*—lion's tooth) or of ground ivy, made and used in the same way, with prayer said over it before drinking.

For the Blood

The juice of carrots boiled down is admirable
for purifying the blood.

For Burns

There is a pretty secret to cure a burn without a scar:
"Take sheep's suet and the rind of the elder tree,
boil both together, and the ointment will cure
a burn without leaving a mark."

They say in Shark Island that any person who rubs their tongue
over a lizard's back will be given power to cure a burn by applying
the tongue to the part affected.

It is believed in the South and West that if a person is licked by the
lizard, they will never suffer from burns, and can even heal them in
another by touch; for a person one day having trod on a lizard,
found that he had acquired this power by the contact.

In modern times, a plaster of potatoes, scraped as for starch, is constantly applied for a burn and gives great ease. Fried cabbage leaves are also used by the people to deaden the pain; but a plant of house leek affixed to the thatch of the roof should not be forgotten, as this preserves the inmates of the cabin from scalds, burns, and the danger of fire as long as it remains untouched.

Blow upon the burn three times, repeating the words:
Two angels sat upon a stone,
One was Fire, the other Frost,
Praise Father, Son, and Holy Ghost.

For Contusions

Heat a great stone in the fire, and, when red hot, throw it into water, and bathe the bruise with the liquid. Repeat this treatment twice a day, always first heating the stone, and the cure is certain in a few days.

For Convulsions

Clippings of the hair and nails of a child tied up in a linen cloth and placed under the cradle will cure convulsions.

FOR DEPRESSION OF HEART

When a person becomes low and depressed and careless about everything, as if all vital strength and energy had gone, they are said to have received a fairy blast. And blast-water must be poured over them by the hands of a fairy doctor while saying, "In the name of the saint with the sword, who has strength before God and stands at his right hand." Great care being taken that no portion of the water is profaned. Whatever is left after the operation must be poured on the fire.

FOR DYSENTERY

Woodbine and maiden hair, pounded and boiled in new milk with oatmeal and taken three times a day, the leaves afterward burned, is a cure for dysentery.

For Dyspepsia

Fix a small piece of candle on a penny piece, then lay the patient on their back and place the penny on the region of the stomach; light the candle, and over all place a well-dried tumbler, where the skin will be drawn up, as in cupping. This is called the lifting of the evil from the body.

For Earache

Some wool taken from a black sheep, and worn constantly in the ear, is a sure remedy for earache.

For the Eyes

The most efficacious treatment for diseases of the eye is a pilgrimage to a holy well, for the blessed waters have a healing power for all ophthalmic ailments and can even give sight to the blind.

Pearls upon the eye are said to be removed by an amber bead, the tenth upon the rosary, rubbed upon the eye; and the wise woman of the village will show the amber bead, with a white substance adhering, which she affirms is the pearl removed by the mystic attraction of the amber.

For Fever

To cure fever, place the patient on the sandy shore when the tide is coming in, and the retreating waves will carry away the disease and leave them well.

These words are said over the patient while their arms are lifted in the form of a cross, and water is sprinkled on their head: "May three things cure thee. May the shadow of Christ fall on thee! May the garment of Christ cover thee! May the breath of Christ breathe on thee! And when I come again thou wilt be healed."

Take a ribbon and tie it tightly round the head of the sick person, saying: "In the name of Father, Son, and Holy Ghost, let the fever go from thy head, and be thou healed."

For Freckles

Anoint a freckled face with the blood of a bull or of a hare, and it will put away the freckles and make the skin fair and clear. The distilled water of walnuts is also a cure.

For a Headache

Measuring the head for nervous headache is much practiced. The measuring doctor has certain days for practicing this art and receives or visits patients on no other occasions. The doctor first measures the head with a piece of tape above the ears and across the forehead, then from ear to ear over the crown of the head, then diagonally across the vertex. After this, he uses strong compression with his hands and declares that the head is "too open." And the doctor mutters certain prayers and charms at the same time. This process is repeated for three days until at last the doctor asserts that the head is closing and has grown much smaller—in proof he shows the measurements; and the cure is completed when he pronounces the head to be "quite closed," on which the headache immediately vanishes and the patient is never troubled by it again.

For Hip Disease

Take three green stones gathered from a running brook between
midnight and morning, while no word is said. In silence it must be
done. Then uncover the limb and rub each stone several times
closely downward from the hip to the toe, saying in Irish—
"Wear away, wear away,
There you shall not stay,
Cruel pain—away, away."

For Inflammation

Nine handfuls of mountain moss, dried on a pan to powder. Nine
pinches of it and nine pinches of the ashes from the hearth to be
mixed in whey, taken every Tuesday and Thursday.

For Jaundice

The homeopathic adepts among the Irish doctors always employ yellow medicines for the jaundice, such as saffron, turmeric, sulphur, and even yellow soap. The allopathic method employs other remedies, especially the leaves of the Barbary Fig tree, which is held to be a specific remedy, if brewed to a strong drink, and taken every morning, fasting, for nine days in succession.

The fairy doctors use the following cure:
Nine young shoots from the root of an ash tree are cut down. These are placed in a bottle, which is then buried in a secluded spot, the patient not being allowed to see it.
As long as the bottle remains in the ground, the patient is safe from the disease; but should it be broken, they will have a relapse and probably die from mental emotion caused by fear of the result before many days are over.

For the Measles

This is to be repeated three times, kneeling at a cross,
for three mornings before sunrise, and the child will be cured
by the Sunday following:
"The child has the measles," said John the Baptist.
"The time is short till he is well," said the Son of God.
"When?" said John the Baptist.
"Sunday morning, before sunrise," said the Son of God.

For the Liver Complaint

The leaves of plantain, wild sage, the shamrock, and Golden Dock leaf with valerian and the flower of the daisy, are to be plucked by the person before sunrise, and fasting on Mondays and Wednesdays while Hail Mary is said, and the Paternoster; all these are to be boiled and strained, and the herbs afterward to be carefully burned. A glassful of the liquor is to be taken twice a day.

For the Mumps

Wrap the child in a blanket, take it to the pigsty, rub the child's head to the back of a pig, and the mumps will leave and pass from the child to the animal.

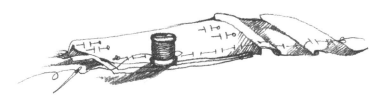

Take nine black stones gathered before sunrise, and bring the patient with a rope around their neck to a holy well—not speaking all the while. Then cast in three stones in the name of God, three in the name of Christ, and three in the name of Mary. Repeat this process for three mornings and the disease will be cured.

For the Red Rash

The red rash is cured by applying unsalted butter to the part affected while the Ave Maria is said. Also the blood of a hare is very efficacious if applied to the skin with a red rag, and the rag afterward buried.

For Rheumatism

The bone of the haddock that lies under the mark of Christ's fingers is always to be carried in the pocket. This bone has many other virtues, and always works good to the owner; but it must not be exhibited, and it should never be lent or touched except by the owner.

Rheumatism was chiefly cured by stroking, and all remedies that acted on the imagination, such as lying in a saint's bed, mesmeric charms, and incantations, were deemed most effectual. Latin words were used as charms, sewn up in a bag and carried in the pocket, tied round the hind legs of a hare. An eel skin had great virtue when placed on the chest, or tied round the knee. Forge water had many virtues and could allay rheumatic pains; potato water, used hot, with the froth on, was also helpful.

For a Stitch in the Side

Rub the part affected with unsalted butter, and make the sign of the cross seven times over the place.

For Stomach Disorders

A bunch of mint tied round the wrist is a sure remedy.

For a Stye on the Eyelid

Point a gooseberry thorn at it nine times, saying, "Away, away, away!" and the stye will vanish presently and disappear.

The tail of a black cat, if rubbed over the eye, will affect a speedy cure. It is good, also, to point nine thorns in succession at the eye, without touching it, throwing away each one after use over the left shoulder.

For Toothache

Carry in your pocket the two jawbones of a haddock; for ever since the miracle of the loaves and fishes, these bones are an infallible remedy against toothache, and the older they are the better, as nearer the time of the miracle.

To avoid toothache, never shave on a Sunday.

The tooth of a dead horse rubbed over the jaw will also be found effective to ease the pain of an ailing tooth.

To Remove Warts

Tie up some pebbles in a bag with a piece of silver money and throw it on the road; whoever finds the bag and keeps the money, to them the warts will go and leave you forever. Also, steal a piece of meat and apply it raw to the warts; then bury it in the ground, and as the meat decays, the warts will disappear. But the charm is of no use unless the meat is stolen, and no one should see you either stealing or burying it.

For Weakness

A black spider laid as a sandwich between two slices of bread with
butter and eaten—one every morning—will be found a great
strengthener of the body.

For Whooping Cough

For whooping cough, a lock of hair, cut from the head of a person
who never saw their father, is to be tied up in a piece of red cloth
and worn round the neck.

Take a mug of water from a running stream, against the current;
give the child a drink, then throw the rest away with the current;
repeat this for three mornings before sunrise, and the cure will
be perfected.

Mystic Charms, Spells
&
Incantations

The ancient druidic charms and invocations continued to hold their power over the people, who believed in them with undoubting faith. No doubt, in pagan times, the invocations were made in the names of Baal and Ashtoreth, and by the power of the sun, the moon, and the winds; but the Christian converts, while still retaining the form of the ancient charms, substituted the names of the Trinity and the words of the Christian ritual as still more powerful in effecting cures.

For Safety

Pluck ten blades of yarrow, keep nine, and cast the tenth away for tithe to the spirits. Put the nine in your stocking, under the heel of the right foot, when going a journey, and the evil one will have no power over you.

How to Have Money Always

Kill a black rooster, and go to the meeting of three crossroads where a murderer is buried. Throw the dead bird over your left shoulder then and there, after nightfall, in the name of the devil, holding a piece of money in your hand all the while. And ever after, no matter what you spend, you will always find the same piece of money undiminished in your pocket.

To Tame a Horse

Whisper the creed in his right ear on a Friday
and again in his left ear on a Wednesday.
Do this weekly till he is tamed; for so he will be.

To Attract Bees

Gather foxglove, raspberry leaves, wild marjoram, mint, chamomile, and valerian; mix them with butter made on May Day, and let the herbs also be gathered on May Day. Boil them all together with honey; then rub the vessel into which the bees should gather, both inside and out, with the mixture; place it in the middle of a tree, and the bees will soon come. Foxglove, or 'fairy fingers,' is called 'the great herb' from its wondrous properties.

To Find Stolen Goods

Place two keys on a sieve in the form of a cross. Two men hold the sieve, while a third makes the sign of the cross on the forehead of the suspected party and calls out their name loudly three times over. If innocent, the keys remain stationary; but if guilty, the keys revolve slowly round the sieve, and then there is no doubt as to who is the thief.

For a Wound

Close the wound tightly with the two fingers, and repeat these
words slowly:
"In the name of the Father, Son, and Holy Mary. The wound was
red, the cut was deep, and the flesh was sore; but there will be no
more blood, and no more pain, till the blessed Virgin Mary bears a
child again."

For a Wound that Bleeds

Place the finger on the spot where the blood flows, and say: "A child
was baptized in the river Jordan; and the water was dark and muddy,
but the child was pure and beautiful. In the name of the God and of
the Lord Christ, let the blood be staunched." And if the patient have
faith, so it will be.

For Protection Against the Plague

"O star of heaven, beloved of the Lord, drive away the foul
constellation that has slain the people with the wound of dreadful
death. O star of the sea, save us from the poison breath that kills,
from the enemy that slays in the night. Amen."

Against Drowning

"May Christ and his saints stand between you and harm.
Mary and her Son.
St. Patrick with his staff.
Martin with his mantle.
Bridget with her veil.
Michael with his shield.
And God over all with his strong right hand."

In Time of Battle

"O Mary, who had the victory over all women, give me victory now over my enemies, that they may fall to the ground as wheat when it is mown."

Against Ill Luck

The most powerful charm against ill luck is a horseshoe made red-hot, then tied up at the entrance door and never after touched or taken down.

Against the Evil Eye

This is a charm Mary gave to St. Bridget, and she wrote it down and hid it in the hair of her head, without deceit:

"If a fairy or a man or a woman hath overlooked thee, there are three greater in heaven who will cast all evil from thee into the great and terrible sea. Pray to them, and to the seven angels of God, and they will watch over thee. Amen."

To avert the evil eye from a child or animal, it is necessary to spit upon the child or animal on entering a cabin; and if a stranger looks fixedly and admiringly on a child, they are at once requested to spit upon the child; this saving process being perhaps unknown to him, or if he should not understand Irish, and omit the rite that preserves from evil, then the old mother will rise up from her seat by the fire and perform the ceremony herself, that so good luck may not depart from the house.

Vervain and the mountain ash are the best preservatives for cattle against witchcraft. Some should be tied round the cow's horns and tail; then no fairy or witch can do harm while the herbs of power are on them.

FOR LOVE

Philters, love powders, and charms to procure affection were frequently used in Ireland, and the belief in them existed from the most ancient times. The bardic legends have frequent allusions to love charms; but the most awful of all is the dead strip. Girls have been known to go to a graveyard at night, exhume a corpse that had been nine days buried, and tear down a strip of the skin from head to foot; this they manage to tie round the leg or arm of the man they love while he sleeps, taking care to remove it before his awaking. And so long as the girl keeps this strip of skin in her possession, secretly hidden from all eyes, so long will she retain the man's love.

To Win Her Love

A charm of most desperate love, to be written with a raven's quill in the blood of the ring finger of the left hand:
"By the power that Christ brought from heaven, mayest thou love me! As the sun follows its course, mayest thou follow me. As light to the eye, as bread to the hungry, as joy to the heart, may thy presence be with me, O woman that I love, till death comes to part us asunder."

To Cause Love

Ten leaves of the hemlock dried and powdered and mixed in food or drink will make the person you like love you in return.

Keep a sprig of mint in your hand till the herb grows moist and warm, then take hold of the hand of the person you love, and they will follow you as long as the two hands close over the herb. No invocation is necessary; silence must be kept between the two parties for ten minutes to give the charm time to work with due efficacy.

If a potion is made up of herbs, it must be paid for in silver;
but charms and incantations are never paid for,
or they would lose their power. A present, however,
may be accepted as an offering of gratitude.

For Faithfulness

This is a charm I set for love; a woman's charm of love
and desire; a charm of God that none can break—
"You for me, and I for thee and for none else;
your face to mine, and your head turned away from all others."
This is to be repeated three times secretly,
over a drink given to the one beloved.

LOVE DREAMS

The girl who wishes to see her future husband must go out and
gather certain herbs in the light of the full moon of the new year,
repeating this charm—
"Moon, moon, tell unto me
When my true love I shall see?
What fine clothes am I to wear?
How many children shall I bear?
For if my love comes not to me,
Dark and dismal my life will be."
Then the girl, cutting three pieces of clay from the sod with a black-
hafted knife, carries them home, ties them up in the left stocking
with the right garter, places the parcel under her pillow, and dreams
a true dream of the man she is to marry and of all her future fate.

An Elixir of Potency

Gather two ounces of cochineal, one ounce of gentian root, two drachmas of saffron, two drachmas of snakeroot, two drachmas of salt of wormwood, and the rinds of ten oranges. The whole is to be steeped in a quart of brandy and kept for use.

Malefic Charms

Not only are charms and incantations employed for curing disease, but they are also used to induce disease and death in the form of maledictions and curses and in the name of the evil one.

A sheaf of corn is sometimes buried with a certain form of dedication to Satan, in the belief that as the corn rots in the ground, so will the person wither away who is under the curse.

Omens & Prophecies

Auguries and prophecies of coming fate may also be obtained from the flight of birds, the motion of the winds, from sneezing, dreams, lots, and the signs from a verse of the Psalter or Gospels. The peasantry attach great importance to the first verses of St. John's Gospel, and maintain that when the rooster crows in the morning, it is repeating these verses (from the first to the fourteenth), and if we understood the language of animals and birds, we could often hear them quoting these same verses.

A charm against sickness is an amulet worn round the neck, enclosing a piece of paper, on which is written the first three verses of St. John's Gospel.

Omens That Forebode Evil

To stick a penknife in the mast of a boat when sailing is
most unlucky.

To meet a man with red hair, or a woman with a red petticoat, the
first thing in the morning.

To have a hare cross your path before sunrise.

To pass a churn and not give a helping hand.

It is unlucky to pass under a hempen rope;
the person who does so will die a violent death,
or is fated to commit an evil act in afterlife,
so it is decreed.

To take away a lighted sod on May Days or churning days;
for fire is the most sacred of all things,
and you take away the blessing from the house along with it.

It is unlucky and a bad omen to carry fire out of a house
where anyone is ill.

If a chair falls as a person rises, it is an unlucky omen.

If the ear itches and is red and hot, someone is speaking ill of you.

A hen that crows is very unlucky and should be killed; very often
the hen is stoned, for it is believed that she is bewitched by
the fairies.

If a man is plowing, no one should cross the path of the horses.

It is unlucky to steal a plow,
or take anything by stealth from a smith's forge.

When yawning, make the sign of the cross instantly
over the mouth, or the evil spirit will make a rush down
and take up his abode within you.

Never give away water before breakfast,
nor milk while churning is going on.

Never give any salt or fire while churning is going on. To upset the
salt is exceedingly unlucky and a bad omen; to avert evil, gather up
the salt and fling it over the right shoulder into the fire,
with the left hand.

Do not put out a light while people are at supper, or there will be one
less at the table before the year is out.

Amongst fatal signs, the most fatal is to break a looking glass, for then it is certain that someone in the house will die before the year is out. And there is no mode of averting the evil fate.

It is very unlucky to meet a weasel coming toward you in the early morning, and you should at once spit at it, for if it spits at you first, a great danger will fall on you before the sun sets. Yet you must never kill a weasel; it is fatal and will bring sure destruction on yourself, for the whole family of the murdered weasel will take vengeance and cause something dreadful to happen to you within the year.

When changing your residence, it is unlucky to bring a cat with you, especially across a stream, and a red and white cat is particularly ominous and dangerous. If a black cat comes of her own accord to your house, keep her—she is a good spirit. But do not bring her; she must come freely, of her own goodwill.

Whoever kills a robin redbreast will never have good luck were they to live a thousand years.

Omens That Foretell Good Luck

The cricket is looked upon as a most lucky inmate of a house, and woe to the person who may happen to kill one, for all the other crickets will meet in general assembly and eat up the offender's clothes as a just retribution for the loss of a friend and relation.

Never disturb the swallows, wherever they may build, and neither remove nor destroy their nests, for they are wise birds and will mark your conduct either for punishment or favor.

If, by accident, you find the back tooth of a horse, carry it about with you as long as you live, and you will never want money; but it must be found by chance.

A purse made from a weasel's skin will never want for money;
but the purse must be found, not given or made.

A coal of fire thrown after the fisherman brings him good fortune.

If the palm of the hand itches, you will be getting money; if the
elbow, you will be changing beds.

To see three magpies on the left hand when on a journey is unlucky;
but two on the right hand is a good omen.

If you hear the cuckoo on your right hand,
you will have luck all the year after.

It is very lucky for a hen and her chickens to stray into your house.
Also it is good to meet a white lamb in the early morning with the
sunlight on its face.

PROPHECIES

Take a piece of the bride's cake and pass it three times through a
wedding ring, then sleep on it, and you will see in a dream the face
of your future spouse.

It is fatal at a marriage to tie a knot in a red handkerchief,
and only an enemy would do it.
To break the spell, the handkerchief should be burned.

The fortunate possessor of the four-leafed shamrock will have luck
in gambling, luck in racing, and witchcraft will have no power over
them. But they must always carry it and never give it away, or even
show it to another.

If anyone is sick in the house, and the cock crows with his head to
the fire, recovery may be expected; but if he crows with his head to
the door, then death is certain.

If one desires to know if a sick person will recover,
take nine smooth stones from running water;
fling them over the right shoulder, then lay them in a turf fire to
remain untouched for one night.
If the disease is to end fatally, the stones in the morning
will emit a clear sound like a bell when struck together.

Superstitions, Secrets
&
Magical Places

A sick person's bed must be placed north and south, not crossways.

When a family has been carried off by fever, the house where they died may be again inhabited with safety if a certain number of sheep are driven in to sleep there for three nights.

An iron ring worn on the fourth finger was considered effective against rheumatism by the Irish peasantry from ancient times.

The ancient arrowheads, called elf stones by the people, are used as charms to guard the cattle.

If you want a person to win at cards, stick a crooked pin in his coat.

If pursued at night by an evil spirit, or the ghost of one dead, and you hear footsteps behind you, try and reach a stream of running water, for if you can cross it, no devil or ghost will be able to follow you.

If a bride steers a boat on the day of her marriage, the winds and the waves have no power over it, be the tempest ever so fierce or the stream ever so rapid.

Fire is the holiest of all things. Walk three times round a fire on St. John's Eve, and you will be safe from disease for all that year.

The cuttings of your hair should not be thrown where birds can find them; for they will take them to build their nests, and then you will have headaches all the year after.

When taking possession of a new house,
everyone should bring in some present,
however trifling, but nothing should be taken away,
and a prayer should be said in each corner of your bedroom
and some article of your clothing be deposited there
at the same time.

Never cut an infant's nails till it is twelve months old, or it will be
light-fingered, and addicted to stealing.

People born in the morning cannot see spirits or the fairy world;
but those born at night have power over ghosts and can see the
spirits of the dead.

The seventh son of a seventh son has power over all diseases,
and can cure them by the laying on of hands; and a son born after
his father's death has power over fevers.

The shoe of a horse or of an ass nailed to the doorpost will bring good luck, because these animals were in the stall when Christ was born and are blessed forevermore. But the shoe must be found, not given, in order to bring luck.

A sick person must not be visited on a Friday, nor by any person who has just quitted a wake and looked upon the dead.

The hair and nails of a sick person must not be cut till after recovery.

Beliefs About Animals

Concerning Dogs

Some very weird superstitions exist in Ireland concerning the howling of dogs. If a dog is heard to howl near the house of a sick person, all hope of recovery is given up, and the patient sinks into despair, knowing that doom is sealed. But the Irish are not alone in holding this superstition. The Egyptians, Hebrews, Greeks, and Romans all looked on the howling of the dog as ominous.

This strange superstition concerning the howling of dogs, when, as is supposed, they are conscious of the approach of the spirit of Death, and see him though he is shrouded and invisible to human eyes, may be found pervading the legends of all nations from the earliest period down to the present time; for it still exists in full force among all classes, the educated as well as the unlettered peasantry; and to this day the howling of a dog where a sick person is lying is regarded in Ireland in all grades of society with pale dismay as a certain sign of approaching death.

Concerning Cats

The Irish have always looked on cats as evil and mysteriously connected with some demoniacal influence. On entering a house the usual salutation is, "God save all here, except the cat." Even the cake on the griddle may be blessed, but no one says, "God bless the cat."

It is believed that the devil often assumes the form of cats. The familiar of a witch is always a black cat, and it is supposed that black cats have powers and faculties quite different from all other of the feline tribe. They are endowed with reason, can understand conversations, and are quite able to talk if they consider it advisable and judicious to join in the conversation. Their temperament is exceedingly unamiable; they are artful, malignant, and skilled in deception, and people should be very cautious in caressing them, for they have the venomous heart and the evil eye and are ever ready to do an injury. Yet the liver of a black cat has the singular power to excite love when properly administered. If ground to powder and infused into potion, the recipient is fated to love passionately the person who offers it and has worked the charm.

Cats were special objects of mysterious dread to the ancient Irish. They believed that many of them were men and women metamorphosed into cats by demoniacal power. Cats also were the guardians of hidden treasure and had often great battles among themselves on account of the hidden gold, when a demon, in the shape of the chief cat, led on the opposing forces on each side and compelled all the cats in the district to take part in the conflict.

Concerning Birds

In all countries superstitions of good or evil are attached to certain birds. The raven, for instance, has a worldwide reputation as the harbinger of evil and ill luck. The wild geese portend a severe winter; the robin is held sacred, for no one would think of harming a bird who bears on his breast the blessed mark of the blood of Christ; while the wren is hunted to death with intense and cruel hate on St. Stephen's Day.

THE MAGPIE

While there is no Irish name for the magpie, it is often called *Francagh*, meaning a Frenchman. While many people do not consider the magpie to be evil, meeting one alone in the morning is considered bad luck. However, meeting more than one is a sign of good fortune, according to an old rhyme that says—
"One for sorrow,
Two for Mirth,
Three for Marriage,
Four for a Birth."

The Wren

The wren is mortally hated by the Irish; on one occasion, when the Irish troops were approaching to attack a portion of Cromwell's army, the wrens came and perched on the Irish drums, and their tapping and noise aroused the English soldiers, who fell on the Irish troops and killed them all. Ever since, the Irish hunt the wren on St. Stephen's Day, and teach their children to run it through with thorns and kill it whenever it can be caught. A dead wren was also tied to a pole and carried from house to house by boys who demanded money; if nothing was given, the wren was buried on the doorstep, which was considered a great insult to the family.

The Cuckoo & Robin Redbreast

It is very unlucky to kill the cuckoo or break its eggs, for it brings fine weather; but most unlucky of all things is to kill the robin redbreast. The robin is God's own bird, sacred and holy, and held in the greatest veneration because of the beautiful tradition among the people, that it was the robin that plucked out the sharpest thorn that was piercing Christ's brow on the cross; and in so doing, the breast of the bird was dyed red with the Savior's blood, and so has remained ever since a sacred and blessed sign to preserve the robin from harm and make it beloved of all men.

THE CRICKET

Crickets are believed to be enchanted. People do not like to express an exact opinion about them, so they are spoken of with great mystery and awe, and no one would venture to kill them. But they are by no means evil; on the contrary, the presence of the cricket is considered lucky; their singing keeps away the fairies at night, who are always anxious to have the whole hearth left clear for themselves, that they may sit round the last embers of the fire and drink the cup of milk left for them by the farmer's wife. The crickets are supposed to be hundreds of years old, and their talk, could we understand it, would no doubt be most interesting and instructive.

The Weasel

Weasels are spiteful and malignant, and old withered witches sometimes take this form. It is extremely unlucky to meet a weasel the first thing in the morning; still it would be hazardous to kill it, for it might be a witch and take revenge. Indeed, one should be very cautious about killing a weasel at any time, for all the other weasels will resent your audacity and kill your chickens when an opportunity offers. The only remedy is to kill one chicken yourself, make the sign of the cross solemnly three times over it, then tie it to a stick hung up in the yard, and the weasels will have no more power for evil, nor the witches who take their form, at least during the year, if the stick is left standing; but the chicken may be eaten when the sun goes down.

THE USES OF HERBS

The hazel tree has many virtues. It is sacred and powerful against the devil's wiles, and has mysteries and secret properties known to the wise and the adepts. It was by the use of a hazel wand that St. Patrick drove out the serpents from Ireland, one only escaping who plunged into the Great Lake at Killarney and remains there to this day, crying to be released. And with a hazel stick, a person can draw a circle around them, within which no evil thing can enter—fairy, demon, serpent, or evil spirit. But the stick must be cut on May Morning, and before sunrise, to make it powerful.

Of all herbs the yarrow is the best for cures and potions. It is even sewn up in clothes as a preventive of disease.

All herbs pulled on May Day Eve have a sacred healing power, if pulled in the name of the Holy Trinity; but if in the name of Satan, they work evil. Some herbs are malefic if broken by the hand. So the plant is tied to a dog's foot, and when he runs, it breaks without a hand touching it and may be used with safety.

There are several herbs that nothing natural or supernatural can injure; they are vervain, Saint-John's-wort, speedwell, eyebright, mallow, and yallow. But they must be pulled at noon on a bright day, near the full moon, to have full power.

The willow is thought to have a soul in it which speaks in music; for this reason the Irish harps were generally made of the wood.

The juice of deadly nightshade, distilled and given in a drink, will make the person who drinks believe whatever you will to tell them and choose for them to believe.

When children are pining away, they are supposed to be fairy-struck, and the juice of twelve leaves of foxglove may be given.

A bunch of mint tied round the wrist keeps off infection and disease.

The rowan tree is very sacred, and branches of it should be hung on May Morning over the child's cradle, and over the churn and the door, to keep away evil spirits and evil hands.

Whoever has the four-leafed shamrock has good luck in all things. They cannot be cheated in a bargain, nor deceived; they will prosper in whatever they undertake. It enlightens the brain and makes one see and know the truth; and by its aid wondrous things can be done.

Great virtue is attributed to the briar, especially in cases of a sprain or dislocation; the species bearing a reddish flower being the best for use.

The buds of the briar are used in spring (and the roots in winter) to make a refreshing drink for the sick. The roots are boiled for twelve hours in an earthen vessel, then a small cupful of the liquid is administered frequently to the patient, who, after some time, falls into a deep sleep from which they will awake perfectly cured.

TRADITIONS—THE FOLK DAYS

May Day in old time was the period of greatest rejoicing in Ireland. It was a festival of dances and garlands to celebrate the resurrection of nature, as November was a time of solemn gloom and mourning for the dying sun. The year was divided into these two epochs, symbolizing death and resurrection, and the year itself was expressed by a word meaning "the circle of the sun," the symbol of which was a hoop, always carried in the popular processions, wreathed with the rowan and the marsh marigold, and bearing, suspended within it, two balls to represent the sun and moon, sometimes covered with gold and silver paper.

A number of ancient traditions circle especially around May Day, called in Irish *La-Bel-Taine* (the day of the sacred Baal fire). In the old pagan times, on May Eve, the druids lit the great sacred fire at Tara, and as the signal flames rose up high in the air, a fire was kindled on every hill in Erin, till the whole island was circled by a zone of flame. It is a saying among the Irish, "Fire and salt are the two most precious things given to man." Fire, above all, was held sacred by them, as the symbol of deity and the mystic means of purification, and three things were never given away by them on May Day—fire, milk, or butter—for this would be to give away luck. No one was permitted to carry a lighted sod out of the house, or to borrow fire in any way. And no strange hand was allowed to milk the cow, for if the first can were filled in the name of the devil there would be no more milk that year for the family—it would all be secretly taken away by the fairies.

THE FIRST THREE DAYS OF MAY

The first three days of May were very dangerous to cattle, for the fairies had then great power given them of the evil one; therefore they were well guarded by lighted fires and branches of the rowan, and the milkmaid made the sign of the cross after milking, with the froth of the milk. Nothing else was so effective against witches and demons.

During the first three days of May, also, it was necessary to take great precautions against the fairies entering the house, for once they gained admittance, they worked mischief. They would come disguised as old women or wayfarers in order to steal a burning coal—a most fatal theft—or to carry off the herbs of power that were always gathered on May Morning with the dew on them. But the best preventive against fairy or demon power was to scatter primroses on the threshold, for no fairy could pass the flower, and the house and household were left in peace, though all strangers were looked upon with great suspicion.

The cattle also are still singed along the back with a lighted wisp of straw, and a bunch of primroses is tied to the cow's tail, for the evil spirits cannot touch anything guarded by these flowers, if they are plucked before sunrise.

But the rowan tree is the best preservative against evil; if a branch be woven into the roof, the house is safe for a year at least, and if mixed with the timber of a boat, no storm will upset it, and no man be drowned in it for the next twelve months.

Hallowtide

The ancient Irish had two great divisions of the year, *Samradh* and *Geimradh*—summer and winter—corresponding to the May and November of our calendar. One represented the resurrection of nature and all things to life; the other the descent of all things to darkness and death.

Saman, or Hallow Eve, was considered the summer end, the first day of winter, when the Sun God entered the kingdom of death; therefore, on that night of gloom, the great sacred fire was lighted on every druid altar to guide him on his downward path; and the druid priests sacrificed a black sheep and offered libations to the dead who had died within the year.

Saman was a weird season of dread and ill omen; for this reason November was called by the Irish "the month of mourning." Then it was said that Baal, the lord of death, summoned before him the souls of the dead to receive judgment for the works done in the human life; and on the vigil of *Saman*, or Hallow Eve, the dead had strange power over the living, and could work them harm and take revenge for any wrong done to them while they lived. Even now, according to the popular belief, it is not safe to be near a churchyard on Hallow Eve, and people should not leave their homes after dark, or the ghosts would pursue them. For on that one night of the year, power is given to the dead, and they rise from their graves and go forth amid the living, and can work good or evil, no man hindering; and at midnight they hold a festival like the fairies of the hill, and drink red wine from fairy cups, and dance in their white shrouds to fairy music till the first red dawn of day. Hallow Eve is the great festival of the dead, when their bonds are loosed, and they revel with mad joy in the life of the living. And if on that night you hear footsteps following you, beware of looking round; it is the dead who are behind you, and if you meet their glance, assuredly you must die.

Garland Sunday
(The first Sunday in September)

This was a great festival with the people from the most ancient times and was devoted by the Irish to solemn rites in honor of their dead kindred. The garland, or hoop, was decorated the night before with colored ribbons, but the flowers that encircled it were not plucked till the morning of the great day, and only unmarried girls were allowed to gather the flowers and wreathe the garland, for the touch of a married woman's hand in the decorations was deemed unlucky. Then all the company proceeded to the churchyard, the finest young man in the village being chosen to carry the garland. From the topmost hoop, some apples were suspended by their stalks, and if one dropped off during the procession, it was considered a lucky omen for the garland-bearer, a prophecy of long life and success in love; but if an apple fell after the garland was set up in the graveyard, it was looked on as a sign of ill luck and coming evil, especially to those who were dancing at the time; for a dance always closed the festival, after prayers were said, and flowers were strewn, with weeping and wailing, over the recent graves. The Irish nature passes lightly from sorrow to mirth, and the evening ended in feasting and dances, while the garland of hospitality was offered to the mourning strangers, who had come, perhaps, a long distance to do honor to their dead kindred.

Index